FACES ARE THREE
OF VIRTUOSITY

Also by Michael André Fath

Published by iUniverse

Novels

The Girls of Yesterday

The Village Squires – Tales of Mayhem and Revenge

Poetry

Reflections of Darkness and Light

Amor est Conceptualis

28 Benedizioni di Rita

FACES ARE THREE
OF VIRTUOSITY

How to discover and develop
your inner creative-genius

Michael André Fath

FACES ARE THREE OF VIRTUOSITY
HOW TO DISCOVER AND DEVELOP YOUR INNER CREATIVE-GENIUS

iUniverse books may be ordered through booksellers or by contacting:

iUniverse
1663 Liberty Drive
Bloomington, IN 47403
www.iuniverse.com
1-800-Authors (1-800-288-4677)

ISBN: 978-1-5320-1457-4 (sc)
ISBN: 978-1-5320-1456-7 (hc)
ISBN: 978-1-5320-1455-0 (e)

Print information available on the last page.

iUniverse rev. date: 12/29/2016

Contents

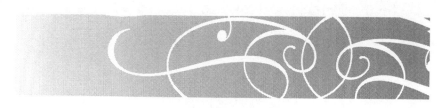

Preface

This is a treatise on discovering and developing one's inner creative genius.

Your artistic life can begin NOW...not yesterday, not five years ago, but today!

I got my first tattoo when I turned 40. I figured I had thought about it quite enough, well, 22 years, to be exact.

Thing is, I hid it from my mom for TWO YEARS, as I knew, even at my age, I would catch a world of grief from her, as I am the oldest of three sons and supposedly the most responsible.

She said to me one day, "I know about your tattoo, your brother Eddie ratted you out. You always wear short-sleeved t-shirts, rolled up, and what do you think after two years of long-sleeved shirts?"

Well, that was the first of several, all now most prominently on display when I go see her.

This is a simple metaphor of beginning what one has always wanted to do, but just never got around to it.

Now, tattoos are easy (at least for some of us), but poetry, playing an instrument, writing a novel, short story or even a technical essay, starting some kind of athletic endeavor, such as a martial art, learning how to sing (pop, rock, blues, classical, jazz), finally becoming the yoga instructor you always wanted to be, taking your first acting class, learning how to box, etc., are all a bit more complicated, but very possible.

This book is not the obvious "all it takes is the first step…" that simply is much too apparent and in truth, more complicated than it may seem.

Rather, I will explain my "concept of three" and illustrate how this essentially works with any creative genre, and very quickly put, this means breaking down your artistic project into three basic and fundamental facets, or corners of a triangle, if you will. All three are continuously in touch with each other at all times (like the recycling symbol), so they will "feed off one another". If your initial breakdown becomes four aspects, then one essential part is always out of touch with another and this eventually becomes a subtle hindrance in one's development.

Of course, there are many features of any creative endeavor, but one will need to develop them as "off-shoots" of your original triangle, as I will present.

Quite a few of my personal clients are either owners or executives of million and even billion dollar companies, extremely successful attorneys, entrepreneurs and working people that all desire a creative escape from their professional realities.

They all need and, more importantly, want to find the time to either study guitar, train in a martial art or finally write that book that has always eluded them; some of them do more than one of these and have been with me for years.

How does one truly reach his or her creative genius?

All it takes is a simple desire or even an inventive idea and the willingness to let it develop. Easier said than done, to be sure, but the real possibility can entice nearly anyone to bring this to fruition.

I am known throughout the world as a virtuoso rock (and, for a period, jazz) guitarist. I achieved this by starting my "concept of three" during my last two years of college and, upon turning pro just after graduation, continuing passionately.

For example, and I will explain in much greater detail later, in music the big three are: 1) repertoire, 2) technique and 3) harmony (theory). Now playing anything: a popular song, a classical etude, a 12-bar blues progression, a rock standard, etc. should be EVERYONE'S ultimate goal, but it does require some technical proficiency and maybe just a minimal amount of harmonic knowledge to achieve this.

The way to do this is set your goal (the repertoire piece) and use just enough of the other two facets to facilitate your desired result. This is helped immensely through great private instruction, and I will discuss how to find exactly that!

Same thing goes for creative writing, which is no different than any innovative genre. Take poetry, for example; you will build your basic "three" once again and I'll strongly suggest: 1) theme (such as, possibly, places and events of growing up), 2) your conceptual and stylistic tendencies (rhyming, more prose-like, acrostic, continuous flow, etc.), and 3) philosophical approach...love, hate, desire, history (truth or revisionist), etc.

Whether writing that first story, sci-fi novella, or even a full-blown narrative, these "principles of three" will factor in greatly.

I am existent proof of this; having recorded and produced hundreds of songs and albums, written three books of poetry and two novels (with more on the way), and finally developing into the world-class martial artist I'd always dreamed of.

As said, "Faces Are Three, Of Virtuosity".

Michael André Fath
March 2016

Dedication

My "concept of three", in its multitudes of professional practice, and even ritual, is something I've always known, somehow, but often inexplicable, if you want to get right down to it.

Examples of my vocational efforts and successes will illustrate this theoretical and philosophical premise, but I have to confess that it's more natural feel than anything so perceptible.

Yes, in this volume I will directly break down obvious and tangible methods of practice, but from where all of this ascended, I can only trust my faith.

The Christian doctrine of the Trinity holds that God is three entities: the Father, the Son, and the Holy Spirit. Very simply put, one God in three Divine Persons.

And so, I most respectfully dedicate this to the basis of my entire creative existence, The Holy Trinity.

And, by the way, this is no coincidence!

Michael André Fath

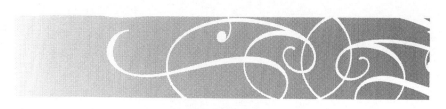

Thanks

To all that actually take the time to not only read this, but contemplate the reasons why we're here for this particular "go 'round" on terra firma, I thank you.

As well, my daughters Jade and Sierra; my brother Vic and mom Elizabeth; my love Rita Conestabile; Rick Davis; Mike Waddell; Russell Anderson; Doc Keith Belote; Doc Kevin Ryan; Doc Millie Nandedkar; Doc Anne Ma; Stilson Greene; Ed Solomon; Linda Hayes; Jim Spruell; Chris Neubauer and Corey Holland; Tommy McCarthy; Prescott Engle; Tom Bateman; Stacy Carroll; my cousin Georgia; Steve Cummins; my students; and, my very best friends.

And very importantly, to all of those that have supported my literature adventures these past several years...I am forever in your debt!

Lastly, and most significantly, I thank God!

Chapter One

Passion is youth, and youth is passion.

These words I've lived by for my entire adult life! What exactly makes one passionate? Answer this honestly, and do something about it.

What creative genre has previously grabbed your heart, at any time of your life? We all need periodic "flashes of youth"...so what used to make you smile?

Nostalgia can be a very powerful motivator, but it can also rip you apart, if you do not apply your years of wisdom to said encounters.

Situational awareness, even in creative expression, is everything. Try to remember that English class where that one poem touched your soul. Attempt to recall when that rock and roll song (THE BEATLES, most likely) completely blew you away. Try to recollect when an athletic feat made the world seem all right. Evoke, if possible, the novel that changed your life at some point.

All of us, if we have an ounce of romanticism, have written a poem in our lives; whether a simple first attempt for an early crush in grade school, something that had been issued in a school periodical, or contest of some sort. It is very possible to not only fill the desire to write verse, but actually get your ideas published!

The very same thing goes in writing a novel, especially for those that are fans of that particular creative writing genre.

It is also truly possible to achieve a 2nd genesis at different stages of one's life...your 3rd, 4th, 5th, etc., as well, and is entirely up to you.

In this book I will present not only my theoretical "concept of three" but several case studies of very successful men and women entrepreneurs that have made it their collective point of starting something creative and most definitely apart from, and outside of, their respective business genres.

As well, I will describe their own particular styles and how I guided them into the "three-aspect-method" to realize their intended artistic endeavors.

You will appreciate that all began with little or no previous training; and, by that, I mean no one was above an intermediate level of a particular genre. In fact, many times one will have a noticeable advantage of beginning from scratch; that of possessing little or no pre-conceived techniques, concepts or philosophies. Not to downplay any sort of real prior training, as much of it is indeed valuable, but many times the proverbial "blank slate" is a proven benefit, and more often than not on a psychological level.

Finding the right motivating force in one's instruction and guidance is of paramount importance. Do your exploration, it's not hard today; we all have the Internet... hello!

Before our fabulous on-line world erupted, my research, for example when I was looking for my first classical guitar instructor many years ago, was done the old-fashioned way; I simply asked anyone and everyone in the mid-Atlantic (USA) that I knew, that was either in the music industry or attached in some fashion, "who's the best classical guitarist that you've seen in concert around here?" It was as simple as that, as those I trusted, especially guitarists, mostly agreed with the same name and I ended up studying with this particular virtuoso for five years, and have remained friends to this day.

Lastly, and this I truly believe, life is much too brief to not explore some of the gifts that have been presented to us by our higher power!

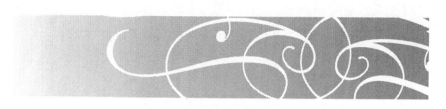

Chapter Two

Case study: Ethan - Engineer and Government Security Specialist.

In the latter phases of my successful profession as an internationally acclaimed rock guitarist, I ventured into the world of jazz. This I needed to do for a brief "career respite", if you will, and felt that I could conquer this genre in much the same fashion that I did in the precarious and fickle world of rock and roll. And, that would be by exhibiting my much regarded technical prowess while being noticeably creative with my interpretations of the world's beautiful and timeless jazz repertoire and original compositions, as well as arrangements of pop and rock classics.

I did have my apprehensions, though; as many of the critics and players in this arena were known snobs that jealously guarded their respective turf from "outsiders", especially rock players, who were often regarded as "uneducated, second class citizens".

I released two solo records and one ensemble disc, all greatly regarded and acclaimed by the powers-that-be in the industry, much to my immense satisfaction and relief.

It was during this time that I was playing a weekly Sunday solo/jazz gig in an exclusive establishment when I observed a very attractive young couple walk by and sit where they could watch and listen.

I noticed that they were paying close attention, especially the guy, and actually commenting to each other on what they were listening to.

On break they introduced themselves and this is when I met Ethan for the very first time. He was an engineer specialist with one of the numerous billion dollar corporations in Northern Virginia (USA), and a lover of music who had previously studied jazz guitar with one of the more notable be-bop players in the mid-Atlantic. However, he was unsatisfied with his progression to date.

Ethan was well informed of my rock history, and enamored with the fact that I could play on a world-class level in two completely separate genres, which was more the exception rather than the rule.

I suggested, "Study with me, and in a few weeks you will absolutely know if this will be the right fit..."

Well, that was eight years ago and is continuing to this very day; every August he books and pays for the next year in advance!

Obviously, Ethan is extremely happy with his progress but it's so much more than that. He has found an escape in his playing. With his company's extremely demanding requirements, plus being the father of four kids and a devoted husband, whenever there's time (and he makes that happen, by the way), Ethan will work on his previous lesson, whether a new standard, or even our forays into the roots rock, bluegrass and country fields. Very often I will create a simple piece to attack; something that can be done in a short amount of time, yet that will sound "professional".

How does the "three concept" fit in with all of this?

I will explain and for you non-musicians reading this, I fully realize this may sound like Greek or Latin, but I can assure you that the hundreds of players I've taught will attest to this methodology.

As well, all of this applies to anything creative and artistic, as you will see.

When I am teaching someone, I will present: 1) the concept (for example, a popular jazz standard); 2) the theory associated (but reducing this to a manageable level) and, 3) the technical exercises needed to fulfill the end result. I also suggest breaking these up with individual focus, and then associating 1 with 2, 2 with 3, 3 with 1, etc., contemplating the inter-relation of all three elements.

After completing said suggestion, I then have one break each of the individual 3-parts down into their own respective "3s".

In this particular case, the concept (1) will become, for example: 1-a) changing a couple of the chord inversions for the melody, 1-b) improvising in different places, and 1-c) related previous stylistic ideas, usually from previous songs.

The theoretical part (2) might become: 2-a) substitution ideas, 2-b) reharmonization concepts, and 2-c) what is used and acceptable in the pro-ranks.

The technical part (3) might become: 3-a) a new arpeggio, 3-b a new scale, and 3-c) applying a unique style of finger-picking more often associated with the best country guitarists...I am absolutely unique with my approach to playing guitar, which has been my greatest acclaim to date!

This same exact approach I will use for 12-measure blues, country, bluegrass solos, etc., and rock progressions and songs, re-formatting the already popular guitar solos into original concepts and melodies.

I have always said to each and every person that's walked into my private studio for a guitar lesson, "All of you process differently, and it is my job to find the singular path that's best suited for YOU, period!"

My intuitive abilities and improvisational skills, especially at a precise moment, have served me well.

Ethan has made such remarkable improvement over the years that he, and as said, continues to study with me. His previous teacher was much too inflexible to pull out of Ethan his own unique skill sets, and that, my readers, is the key to a great instructor, no matter what the artistic endeavor... "It's not about the teacher, it's about the pupil!"

What makes Ethan particularly special, however, is that after just one year into his guitar studies he started to train in Krav Maga (Israel's well-regarded and the world's highest rated system of self-defense) under my tutelage, joining my martial arts academy, and is still going strong.

And even more interesting is that this was his very first venture into the world of martial arts and has recently added to his training TWO other systems and instructors; much the same as if one progressed to a certain level with guitar, say in rock and blues, and then decided to study flamenco music... it all adds to the equation!

Ethan found new life, well into his 40's, and I am most certain that he will continue with all of this newfound energy and reward for years to come.

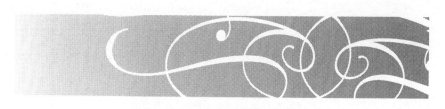

Chapter Three

Writing that first book of poetry.

Yes, all of you have written that poem of faith and love at some point of your life; and, I don't care if it was elementary school (when I happened to start), junior or senior high school, or even college (if you were a late-bloomer). It's human nature and our naturally blessed (for me, by God) and intuitive expression of the most wondrous feeling ever!

I have had, so far, three books of verse published and that are available worldwide: ***28 Benedizioni Di Rita, Amor est Conceptualis, and Reflections of Darkness and Light.***

Like many, I attempted some poetry as a very young boy, wanting to impress upon the girl of my dreams (at that particular time) the depth of my feelings for her.

This has been a re-occurring theme throughout my adult life, as well, and if anyone has ever received such a paean from someone, I need not explain the wondrous psychological and emotional lift from such an encounter.

Now, I was not an English or literature major in college (mine was Kinesiology and Psychology, as I was going to be a physical therapist), and had never actually studied the technical methods involved with this discipline. As well, and to be perfectly honest, I was not the greatest fan of said creative writing genre, but as I experimented with my initial thoughts that turned into actuality, I became more and more interested in the master poets, which concurrently grew with my skill.

The critical acclaim for my poetry has been very rewarding, but I intuitively knew that I was gifted in this arena.

Yes, I had written many songs with lyrics, but that is a different process (at least for me) and I do not personally equate the two; yet, it has been successfully done by others, to be fair, just not my style.

I began with the theme of the book I had in mind to create, and my first title, "**Reflections of Darkness and Light**", accurately portrays the entries involved.

The happier or "light" reflections were soul-lifting, such as: my daughters' singular and collective magnificence, the sublime beauty of a pine tree, the splendor of the Chesapeake Bay, and the exquisiteness of a yellow sundress...I could go on and on.   And, to counter-balance with the unhappier or "darkness" side: losing my younger brother to cancer, losing my dad to same feared disease, being a single father, my favorite season (summer) fading away, the meaning of Memorial Day, my high school best friend's son's suicide, etc., brought much angst and sadness, but ultimately proved to be a very positive and fulfilling catharsis.

Here is an example of a dad's remembrance of giving his two daughters baths and how absolutely wonderful that was, but alas they grow up and this particular phase in life is all but a very fond memory.

From *Reflections of Darkness and Light:*

Little Mermaids ©

The splash of your play shall forever stand fast
Those wondrous moments of three
Sharing peaceful, warm currents blissfully

As you today offer me babes long since passed
I often am saddened of play nevermore
These beautiful two, how truly I adore

A dad's time continuum overwhelmingly vast
Infants then children then girls and now
Women so remarkable, in reverence I bow

Those moments of laughter still unsurpassed
Cascading rivulets of hair wet with glee
I so miss my bath pixies, regretfully

A lesson to be sure and not miscast
Innocence of youth so nostalgic I claim
Treasured forever and ever, I shall remain

Your guardian angel, first and last
Our ritual moments of aqua transcendent
Oh Little Mermaids, how vastly resplendent

And to counterbalance, in this particular volume of poetry, the dark side of life, in my case, needed to be equally qualified. My one year younger brother, Edouard Emile Fath, world-class opera baritone, lost his battle with cancer. These were my thoughts, as I lamented his passing.

From *Reflections of Darkness and Light:*

A Most Cherished Goodbye ©

Anticipation as yet unheard
Paralyzing to be sure
Time gathering life ever so subtly
Never he and I had to endure
I knew this would be the last
And how does one prepare
To share everything from inner being
With only moments to have and spare
A smile greeted my arrival
Breaking my heart yet I pause
Steadfast in demeanor of hope and appeal
To forever champion his cause
My throat clutches as I share
Prayers from many who love
I echo sentiment as fiercely
Masking anger directed above
He laughs for just an instance
Forgetting briefly the pain
And shares his faith and destiny
Offering me his ultimate gain
My younger brother gives thanks
For my lifelong devotion as one
Most cherished sentinel sibling
My tears now undone

Consoling one who will live
Makes me feel less than the man
I ask absolution for weakness
A smile and offering of his hand
My lifelong friend soon shall pass
And leave such profound gifts
Of son, husband, father and voice
Everlasting in my heart he lifts

Often times simply writing things down will alleviate great inner-conflict, and imagine, if you will, the beauty of creatively articulating these thoughts and expressions into something that you are delighted with, and want to share with your loved ones, friends and even the world!

I can attest that it is a truly gratifying experience and something with which your personal growth can exponentially expand, especially from any sort of positive feedback.

To begin, start with a group topic or theme and realize that at anytime this can be altered or even completely changed. It is important to think of a collection of sorts, as uniformity and continuity will greatly facilitate end results; these entries will feed off one another throughout the process.

For example, let's say that you'd like to chronicle the places you've experienced that affected you, either positively or negatively. One could be the Vietnam Memorial, which needs very little discussion. Your personal viewpoint could be one of several: 1) you served in that conflict, 2) you know someone that did, 3) you studied the war in a particular class, 4) you have a Vietnamese wife or related family, 5) you visited the country, etc., etc. This poem could be either an uplifting one or quite the opposite, but BOTH will have meaning and impact.

Here is an example of a man that served in Vietnam, and has his PhD in Psychology, and became my "spiritually adopted father", after taking me under his wing in numerous counseling sessions. His basement is a sanctuary of sorts for him, and I was moved, beyond belief, as to his daily ritual homage to the nine classmates he lost over there.

From *Reflections of Darkness and Light:*

A Warrior's Shrine ©

The river delta, brown and green
Of that beautiful Asian land
Luxuriance intoxicating and benign, yet still
Requiring his steely focus and concern
As with his mates, life possibly tenuous
Anywhere, everywhere, at a moment's turn

Back in "the world", assimilation doubt
At least for this first return
Was it previous reverie or nightmare?
2nd tour in country, a duty request
To verify sights, sounds and smells
With conviction to fellow Marines' his bequest

Surviving again, this time around
Prayers answered, thanks most gracious
Farewell to conflict designed by choice
Another return to his homeland of yore
Body intact, yet mind and soul
Clutching pangs of pressure ne'er before

Years' ritual to his basement, cave of man
Off room iron plates beckon his resolve
Yet before every session, passing by
The Wall with adornment of nine
Ceremonial benediction and love, he salutes all
Departed souls not forgotten, his Valhalla all time

There are a multitude of approaches in writing poetry, and just for now you may either rhyme every other line, do stanzas of four lines with the 1st and 4th rhyming, or do it as an acrostic entry (basically a poem or series of lines in which certain letters, usually the first in each line, form a name, motto, or message when read in sequence), such as using the individual letters of your topic to begin each line to portray your thoughts.

Here is an acrostic example and, again, my girls are the theme.

From *Amor est Conceptualis:*

My Daughters as Women ©

Mature, beyond all anticipation
Youthful, their bloodline causation

Discovering life's numerous ways
As astute as can be, no daze
Uniform in belief, sibling praise
Girls, my chosen quest for all days
"Hers," not "His," focused gaze
True to themselves...lesson, as I raise
Each spirit, uniquely defined to amaze
Resolute, my love, I appraise
"Soul Mates," most meaningful phrase

Agreement between us, when I leave
Seashore spreading of ashes, they bequeath

Women, yet my children forever
Our lifeline ties, no option to sever
My greatest accomplishment, ever
Every morning, prayer my endeavor
Neglecting their needs and love...never

To employ my "three-facet" methodology, keep reminding yourself of: 1) the theme of this collection (various places), 2) your particular stylistic tendencies (and these, in and of themselves, can revolve), and 3) your personal passions (pain, joy, spiritual, physical, psychological, philosophical, etc.).

When inspired, look at this "triangle", re-read what you've previously written, and begin another poem. It is truly that simple, especially if one is motivated enough to see end results.

Most, if not all, successful people have this ability. I know that I do.

Amor Est Conceptualis means Love is Conceptual in Latin, and I followed this theory throughout this entire volume.

Another example of the many types of love is my thanks to the girl that edits all of my poetry, and a close friend.

From *Amor Est Conceptualis:*

My Poetic Sentinel ©

She favors the gift of words, and I readily comply
Offering my various rhyme, for her discerning eye

Friend for many years, and fan of six-string skill
Sent appreciation many times, often love was thrill

As young lady, her countenance would dazzle
And a simple cotton sundress, could frazzle

She flew up and away, but never too far to touch
Still wistful the memories, related emotions and such

First book of poetry, editorial proficiency my request
Fine-tuning author's verse, her touch indeed blessed

And today with second effort, my invitation is the same
Seeking her counsel and passion, heart's peripheral flame

Trusting technical grace, allowing my words to breathe
Her understanding and nature, to protect and to sheathe

I thank you Poetic Sentinel, my art lies in your hand
And love and adoration, for you my friend is grand

My third book of verse was solely focused on a newfound love, someone that completely turned my world around, even when I thought that it could never be done again.

I took the time and my philosophical inspiration to write, write and write.

She is illuminated in numerous ways in this entire volume of verse, and this particular entry describes how I envision her many years later.

From *28 Benedizioni di Rita:*

Fade To An Even Lovelier ©

I have seen your face
10 years from today
I know this, so truly
And yes, I must say

Your face even more
Lovelier than now
Small lines of wisdom
Enlightenment, ciao

I look into Crystal...
Ball in my mind
20/30 years future
This is what I find

My wife, best friend
Even prettier than ever
Her heart and happiness
My most sacred endeavor

Before I got into writing, all I ever wanted was to be the world's greatest rock guitarist, and so I looked at my competition, emulated the players I adored, and then passionately developed my personal "concept of three" attitude to achieve what I coveted.

This was: 1) technical prowess, especially that which was unique to my personal skill sets, 2) individual flair and creativity in delivery, and 3) compositional ability.

As well, my "off-set three" from number 1: concert performance, recording prowess and seminar skills.

In conclusion, finish your collection, even if it takes a year or two, use an editor/friend that you trust, find a great graphic designer, and SELF PUBLISH! This is the way of the world, now; NO ONE wants to take chances anymore, so it's on us to create our own destinies.

When you are holding your very first copy you will know...

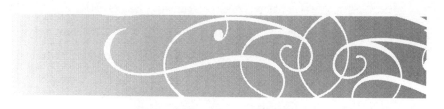

Chapter Four

Case study: Cat – Attorney/Law Firm Owner, and Psychology Masters in Counseling.

I met Cat at a party given by one of my other lawyer clients; both were professional friends, the heads of their respective law firms, and extremely well regarded.

He had told her of his martial arts study with me, which at that time had been approximately four years and still going well, and of how much it had changed his attitude about his own personal self-defense abilities, especially as he was a highly acclaimed gun expert and co-owner of a firearms training facility.

She and I talked for a half hour or so, and was convinced enough to participate with my standard two-hour consulting and introduction session that very next day.

I thought that my aspirations, schedule and routines were complex, but Cat could be the only person I've met that is even busier. Now this may or may not be a detriment to her, but so far the results speak for themselves.

She was totally impressed by our first session, so much so that for the last four years she has scheduled 10 two-hour sessions every single month! As said, she's determined, but just as importantly she is finding a new creative side to herself that previously did not exist.

Cat cautioned me as to her lack of "natural athletic abilities", and I said that it did not matter. We would find a way, somehow, to maximize her strengths and minimize her weaknesses...that's what we do, at least those of us that know how to truly teach. When we're dealing with life-saving techniques, concepts and philosophies, it's just as much mental as physical. In truth, this applies to any kind of educational undertaking.

Her personal "concept of three" was exactly: 1) fitness (and I applied numerous "combative" techniques to achieve this), 2) methods of escaping an assault (a mainstay of my curriculum, especially for women and children), and 3) use of weapons, specifically the collapsible baton (which in our state is legal to conceal and carry) and the knife.

We would revolve through these three concepts, going off into related tangents from time to time, but perfecting her grasp of: 1) Krav Maga, 2) Kali and 3) JuJutsu...which happens to be the conceptual and philosophical basis of my Blue Chip Academy.

When she needed to rehab her minor hip and stomach issues, swimming was one method, with even another "three" added: 1) conditioning with her punches, kicks, etc., 2) wrist and body escapes, and 3) weapons use, but ALL in the water.

Very fun, very focused and very pertinent, to be sure, but accomplishing the rehabilitation that was sorely (no pun intended...well, maybe) needed.

Lastly, Cat is an accomplished business professional in one of the very largest money markets (and tax brackets) in America. The corporate structure in and around the Washington, DC region is insane, with regards to numbers of companies, monies earned and people involved. One of my best friends, who is a realtor, is constantly overwhelmed at the high incomes presented him by clients, especially younger ones, when doing a house transaction.

Cat has plans to continue training, at least until she reaches the coveted Black Belt (she's now green and has a few years in front of her); however, as I told her and for those of us that really know from experience, "that's when training truly begins".

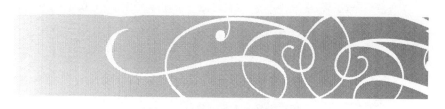

Chapter Five

Can you really write a novel?

When my first narrative **The Girls of Yesterday** was published, I could not begin to tell you how many people came up to me and said, in so many words, "Wow, I cannot believe you wrote a novel. I've always wanted to..."

On one occasion, I was playing a concert with several other acts and one guitarist in particular pulled me aside and asked me when did I ever find the time? I told him that I would write a page or two most mornings and, when truly inspired, might get six to ten written during a rare afternoon that "presented itself".

He still looked incredulous, and so I further explained to this great talent that I had known for years, which is why I actually took the time before a performance, that I simply had an original idea that I truly felt passionate about and slowly but surely developed it.

Now, much easier said than done, however most great things are just exactly that. "Talk is cheap", as they all say.

I had always wanted a sister, whether older or younger, as my two younger brothers stretched my "big brother capacity" to its limits. So, I made one up, a composite of two women that I had adored since childhood, one a cousin, the other a great friend and one-time love, many years previous.

I have two daughters, now 29 and 26, and am well known for being one of the very finest dads on the planet, or at least that's been my most beloved motivation, as I had failed in so many other relationships, and I most desired to create a heroine with my main character.

I also wanted her one-year older brother to rely on her intuition and strength, all the while championing her cause throughout their lives.

From *The Girls of Yesterday:*

Chapter V (excerpt) ©

A brother and sister's relationship can be many, many things. Loretta and I would probably qualify as the distinct minority in terms of what we meant to each other, and more importantly, how we treated one another.

I mean that I do not believe that we represented the "norm". Yes, there are many sibling relationships that are strong and respectful, but ours went beyond anything that most had ever seen, and anything that our close friends and family had been privy to as well.

For starters, when we were toddlers, we were always helping each other; at least this is what mom and dad would constantly remind us throughout our lives. Even though I was a year older than Loretta, she was walking before my slow ass could. I think that I was 20 months of age, doing my level best at holding on to whatever furniture that was available, when Loretta, at her tender age of 8 months and maybe a few days, glided across the floor like some little, cute, curly-haired version of Baryshnikov, waltzing by me in a toddler's version of Ginger Rogers and a stoned-drunk Fred Astaire.

In a few days, she was grabbing me and actually helping me to balance myself and inevitably walk right beside her. I mean that she was my teacher and terra firma before I was two years of age!

There was this sparkle in her eyes as she watched me take my first couple of steps. It's almost as if she was on her mission before she could talk; which brings up another of Loretta's super-baby qualities: her ability to communicate without even speaking. Never mind the fact that she was forming entire sentences by the time that she was 15 months, and of course guiding my linguistic excursions as well!

I know that mom was cognizant of Loretta's abilities to a point, just as dad was all too aware of my deficiencies, not as compared to other very young boys my age, but as balanced along side our little super girl. But this never seemed to matter, as Loretta was so far ahead of "the curve" that I was always given some deference, just based on common sense alone.

My motor and verbal skills gradually caught up with my sister's, and by the time that I was four (she being three), we were playing, talking and even reading on more or less an equal level. Of course, there are many, many different plateaus of achievement in childhood development and just when I would think that I was holding my own, or dare I say it, even starting to surpass my younger rival, Loretta would completely mystify all of us with yet another accomplishment; like the day that she learned how to swim, or rather the day that we knew she could swim...

Now being American/Southern, I am well acquainted with the gothic drama that our region creates, and precisely unlike other parts of our great country. And further, with the ultimate tragic outcome of my novel, I promised myself that I would have evoked out of all who read, every imaginable human emotion, especially tears, both of laughter and pain!

I started my story with my "three concept" squarely in place; 1) the main characters Loretta, Jesse and Jess and their complete love for one another (there are many in this novel, as their interaction and development is a most important aspect of any great journey in literature), 2) college and basketball experience as a main backdrop, and 3) my depicting the wide range of emotional connections with life experiences in general, so as ALL could associate on some level.

As well, my description of the region where everything takes place was a real joy.

From *The Girls of Yesterday:*

Chapter III (excerpt) ©

Indian Summer in the mountains of Virginia is unlike anything else on earth. God's Country is a description used for many of the lovely land and seascapes that He created with a most divine sense of artistic and intuitive ability, and the celestial nobility of these mountains found in Miss Virginia's domain are a tapestry that is as compelling as anything on this planet.

The crystalline smell of the air can invigorate, beyond expectation, the most lifeless of us, and yet the pungent aromas of these alpine leaves, that are still green with summer but ripening with fall in their veins, can so intoxicate one as to rival the most prodigious cocaine/heroin popper found in any drug connoisseur's private reserve.

My own personal feelings aside, as I'm one of those whose lifeblood is synonymous with the sea, there is definitely an atmospheric "pressure" found in those hills that permeates the soul, charges the psyche, and flourishes as an unyielding specter, affecting everything that it touches.

Mountain people, plainly and simply, are unlike any others. The sheer isolation, that is the environmental prerequisite of many of these folks, imparts a certain philosophy of life that separates these people from everyone else, and some of this is good, and some of this is bad.

In these hills, one can certainly feel that freedom in everyday life apart from the "normal" constraints that bind those of us not included in this "hillbilly" society.

Unfortunately, there is also an obvious lack of cultural integration that has a tendency to diminish or even close a lot of healthy minds that are educated in some of these mountainous areas...

A novel can basically be three-fold: 1) completely fictitious, 2) evenly depicted, with truth being half of the story, more or less, and 3) mostly based on fact, such as our wonderful historical novels.

With my first and second novels I used first and third person writing techniques, respectively. Each were, and by design (as I have lived and continue to do so, an extremely colorful life), 1) 50% truth, 2) 25% embellished and 3) 25% purely fiction.

This is my style, plainly and simply, as once I get out of the starting blocks, things seem to flow, and really, why upset a good thing?

Now, and I will be further candid, not everyone can write a novel, nor depict in sentences meaningful enough and interesting enough to develop characters and relationships that will grasp the attention of readers of this literary style.

You will know soon enough. Write your first ten pages and if your close friends will be honest with you, they will say that you either may be onto to something special, which was (thankfully) what happened with yours truly; or kindly let you know that your skills lie elsewhere.

NOTHING WRONG WITH THAT! That's the purpose of this treatise...ALL OF US were given creative genius by God. For most of us, it's our basic desire (and responsibility, as far as I'm concerned), to tap these inner resources at some point in our respective lives, so why not start now?

Lastly, and a very important thing to consider, as well; when searching and experimenting for your particular creative outlet, whatever the case may be, know that previous personal experience and background interest will factor in, usually more than expected.

In my case, I was an avid reader, especially of novels, as far back as I could remember.

My mother was highly educated (a chemist and guidance counselor by trade), and always professed to her three boys the importance of reading and the great "escape" that it provided, especially when life turned upside down.

I took this lesson to heart (I was reading by age two) and read more than any of my friends. When the bookmobile came to my street, and those days are far-gone, the librarian/driver would let me check out two books for the week as opposed to one, as long as I could accurately give her each story's synopsis and a few specific details.

Same thing for my eventual professional guitar experiences; I had loved The Beatles upon first hearing them and had to pursue what had literally clutched my heart and soul.

A real tragedy in life is to deny your inner passions. Many "flat-line" through their time here on earth, for various real and imagined reasons. Yes, being professionally successful can be rewarding to the extent that our families are taken care of, which in itself is most noble; however, to deny your own very spirit, how sad.

Write what you know, and know what you write. In my case, nothing was more apparent for me to create than my second novel *"The Village Squires – Tales of Mayhem and Revenge"*. A rock and roll story of honor, redemption and decent glimpses of fame, which I had lived and breathed for many years; all for which I am extremely thankful, and still going strongly to this day.

From *The Village Squires - Tales of Mayhem and Revenge:*

Chapter Two (excerpt) ©

All four members of the Village Squires, Paul, John, Rocky and Mickey, had more or less grown up together since grade school. Each had come from lower middle class families with both parents working, so the "after school/early evening at home parental chaperoning", that was there for many of their other friends, was virtually non-existent, save for Rocky's big brother Charlie (also the band's first manager, as he drove a very big, honking station wagon that could carry all of their equipment), who was even more prone to delinquency. Paul was an only child, Mickey had two younger brothers, and John, a younger sister.

The fact that Paul and John were slightly older and one grade ahead of Mickey and Rocky did not seem to matter, as these boys had a very natural affinity for one another, quite possibly because of their common and provincial blue-collar upbringing, but in truth more so due to the mutual respect of their various talents and personalities.

As early as junior high, and even with possessing good athletic skills, each of them gravitated towards rock and roll, moving away from all of the team sports so heavily emphasized among their various schoolmates and acquaintances, somehow understanding and even knowing of their early-life destinies, with each being passionately drawn into developing the vocal and instrumental skills necessary to be individually very good and collectively close to outstanding.

The Village Squires moniker fit their youthful spirituality like a glove. The combative nature of each member, whether working out, or even scrapping with others, coupled with their approach to rock and roll music in general, and the Squires in particular, somehow made this name extremely appropriate, almost "gang-like", and quite simply, it was extremely catchy.

From the beginning of their band's existence, there was an obvious electric essence and élan to their shows. While other bands in town were as good, maybe one or two of them with more experience a little better, none had the feel and vibe of the Squires, and anyone that has ever reached a high level of music performance, particularly in rock and roots styles, knows truly that this pulse is the singular most important, almost universal, aspect of this discipline.

By the time Mickey and Rocky were juniors, Paul and John seniors, the Village Squires were really starting to make a name for themselves...

To conclude, if you cannot write in this literary style, then try something else. Maybe even the novella or short story is an answer, as the finish line is much closer.

Most successful authors have either experimented with this form or written several for publication.

All in all, give it your best shot and follow the talents and character traits that motivated you to become the person that you now are.

Even though the full-blown novel may seem out of reach at first, let your story evolve, it just may create a life of its own; quite possibly your own personal experiences will reveal themselves and facilitate this very notion, especially with imaginative characters and their development and interaction.

These very same qualities can all apply across the board... we are who we are.

The great novelist Pat Conroy (and my very favorite of all time) once told me that every time he finished one of his magnificent works, it took a piece of his soul, as the truth in his fiction was quite apparent.

I truly now know what he meant by those very cryptic words, and will always treasure his genius.

The conclusion of *The Village Squires...* was a very real experience of my own, with just enough fantasy thrown in to make me believe and feel.

YOU CAN TOO!

From *The Village Squires - Tales of Mayhem and Revenge:*

Chapter Eighteen (excerpt) ©

Nevertheless, it was the very last show that would forever be etched upon the collective souls of Paul Bayonne, John Wilson, Rockford Reeves and Mickey Franz...lovingly engraved memories making all experiences heretofore more than worthwhile, and perpetually appreciated.

Sheila and Gary Blackstone, Dana and Jack Fortino reserved a front row table that also included Miles Madsen, whom Jack flew in for this event; and, at his further courtesy, a giant bouquet of flowers with several bottles of champagne adorned the front of the stage.

Sitting immediately to their left, at another reserved table, were Barbara Greene, her girlfriend Tanya, Georgie Beauregard and an unknown person, but obviously his friend. Something intuitively told Mickey that this was who had accompanied Georgie that eventful night in Nashville, and when Mickey had looked at both, back and forth, Georgie's wink verified his insight.

Sheila and Barbara had introduced themselves, finally in person, and Lord knows what they shared, but the band suspected it was mutually very satisfying, as they seemed to hit it off extremely well.

Rocky's fiancé, Stephanie, Johnny's new girlfriend (and eventual wife), Trisha, and Paulie's wife, Maria, all were to the immediate right of Jack Fortino, with everyone eventually shoving their three separate tables together, forming one large community setting.

Sandy happened to have a new photo of both children together, and after surreptitiously inscribing it "to aunt Barbie and uncle Georgie, love, André and lil' Doc", presented it to them...one might have thought she had given them the secret to eternal happiness...and maybe she just did, at that!

Lastly, Colonel Dion Neal appeared at the side of the stage, having pre-arranged to be there, and as all four looked over before starting their very first song, he saluted them, grinning like a proud big brother. All four saluted back!

The Village Squires, for the very last time, played and sang their hearts out. By the end, Paulie, Johnny, Rocky and Mickey were in tears, and all in attendance accepting favorably, as it was as real as it gets.

Every single person in the audience witnessed four youthful, yet now middle-aged, guys still believing in each other, after so many years, in exactly the same manner as when they were kids. Their childhood was, if only briefly, visibly put on display for several hundred that night to see, hear and more importantly, share.

Paulie Bayonne, Johnny Wilson, Rocky Reeves and Mickey Franz had come full circle, completing the design that God had expertly crafted for them to receive, understand, rework and ultimately present to the world.

Talented boys? Most would concur.

Magnificent men? Ask any who knew and loved them.

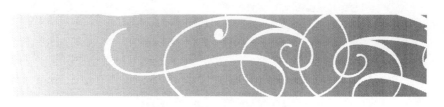

Chapter Six

Case study: Eddie – Insurance Company Owner and Army Special Forces Officer, Ret.

Nine years ago Eddie, through a mutual friend, asked me to produce his debut record. At that time we barely knew each other but I did know that he had been playing around part-time with an acoustic trio, who were, honestly, just a little better than average. His business and family were his focus and music just a pastime, albeit serious enough for Eddie to have taken the time, apart from his band, to write a record's worth of pretty good songs. Plus, he had the financial resources to get it done; in other words, he was extremely serious about this personal and creative side of his.

This was intriguing to me; here Eddie stood, extremely effective in his profession yet willing to take the chance on a fairly large expenditure, with studio time, musicians, engineering and production involved, just to have a professionally completed CD. Well, this was his own inner-voice compelling him to do just that.

Both the engineer, who also was the studio owner (and a well-regarded songwriter and musician), and I helped on arrangements and minor writing editing, but the songs were Eddie's, and his lyrics portrayed a good range of the human spirit and emotional rollercoaster rides that we've all been privileged to have participated.

After the record was finished, with a good 120+ hours having been necessary, Eddie started to study guitar with me on a weekly basis. I had played all of the electric and acoustic guitars on the album (plus bass, mandolin and banjo), and so he had received an "up close and personal" experience with what I was all about, especially within the confines of his own music.

That was eight years ago!

Eddie was, by his very own admission, an average guitar player, but a good singer and songwriter. I would agree, but that was then. Today he is a much greater musician, and working on his THIRD RECORD!

Our approach for the last several years was again three-fold, but a generally focused one at that: 1) his guitar skills, 2) his singing, and 3) his writing. Now, I was his guitar mentor, but all of the aforementioned skill sets are acutely related, and I am always using #2 and #3 to augment #1, even to some of my students' hesitancy at my method; this always proves to be productive, however, and they are always very satisfied.

With regards to his singing and writing evolution, this was a smooth ride, so to speak, as he already was competent in both arenas.

However, his guitar playing development was just short of eye opening. All of this is relative, to be sure, but I cannot tell you how many sincere compliments Eddie has received over these last few years, and they are numerous, trust me.

We followed a very specific three-way attack in his guitar pedagogy, and this was: 1), improving a technique that was a bit unnatural at first, 2) his general, basic theoretical knowledge, and 3) solo construction and improvising ability; rotating, more or less equally, with each category usually focusing on one per week.

Each year would pass and we would evaluate; but in truth, it was his friends and fans that gave him the analysis, whenever he played in public.

Here were are today, and still getting together on a weekly basis. His insurance company has expanded and now Eddie is what we all call today a "major player" in the insurance industry.

He's looking to transition out in the near future and into consulting and developing his other business interests, but one thing is certain, and that is he will be continuing with me (his words) for years to come.

When he first came to me to produce his record, I asked him a simple question, and that was, "Why are you doing this debut record?"

His reply was the patented response, and in so many words, "To get my name out there; or, to have something the radio stations can play; or, to be judged along with others; or, to let my fans have something to take home; or, for posterity..."

All great reactions, all correct answers, but none the philosophically precise one.

And, that would be, "To get to record number two!"

When I said this, the look in his eyes and the smile on his face told me, faithfully, that he got it.

The progress we all can make from one project to the next, is almost impossible to compare to staying the course, being hesitant, and waiting and waiting until one thinks that they are ready.

Part of success is failure, but you cannot be paralyzed by this fear, at least excessively so. I will talk about this, at length, later; and, trust me; I have failed too many times to count on all my fingers and toes.

Eddie is an extremely intelligent and educated man. Also, an honorable one, a bit excessive at times, but aren't we all?

He received an undergraduate degree from a fine West Virginia institution, but his real schooling came from the

Army Special Forces Group, of which he was a stellar member, and, even further, being the father of eight wonderful kids. This is where he learned to cultivate his inner creativity; he had to, to literally save him from himself.

Sound familiar?

He and I have had numerous discussions on national politics, religion, faith, music, local political candidates that we knew personally, our high school and college athletic exploits, our girlfriends of the past and present day partners, the state of affairs in present day America, our mutual friends, writing, performing, etc.

Spirit and energy are very seductive, and this life force that we exude, especially if it's positive, can be as compelling as nearly anything imaginable.

Creative minds think alike, you've all heard this, but I can attest to its virtue.

Find the best player or singer in your immediate region, and take the time to begin your journey.

This is key...START! First step is a challenge, but so worth the effort, and this I can promise you!

Chapter Seven

The fear of failure.

All of us hate to lose but it just may bother me a little less than most in this world and it came to me honestly; however, if we are talking about losing a love, then I am with most of you...it always crushes.

My senior year of high school was an absolute lesson in humility, specifically with my football and basketball teams.

The summer before my final year our high school's student body had literally split because of new zoning and, consequently, a new school, and our respective teams were basically "cut into halves", depleted like never before.

As a result, we lost all but one football game, and every single one of our basketball contests. This was monumentally depressing for many of my teammates, classmates and friends, but somehow I managed to focus on my individual efforts, along with my teams', and played very well; well enough to go on to play college basketball at a very fine institution.

I felt very strongly and deep in my heart that we all were lucky enough to just be able to play; I mean, every single game was so much fun and meaningful to yours truly.

I can distinctly recall being on the gridiron and smelling the cut grass and autumn leaves and thinking of just how glorious all of this really was.

As well, the basketball gymnasium had its very own feel and rhythm, with all of the ubiquitous squeaking sneakers and sweat of its contestants, it made me fully appreciate being good enough to participate in such a wonderful sport.

As a result of losing so many games, I didn't become desensitized but rather even more appreciative of actually participating in such magnificence and thanking God for just the opportunity.

Yes, I was a collegiate basketball player, and our team was very good, but we lost our share and my teammates always asked me why losing didn't crush me, as it did some, and I always would answer that I was fully indebted to God for my fitness, ability and positive outlook on playing another game.

This would serve me extremely well later in life, with personal and business ventures, especially the precarious and extremely unfair (hello) world of professional rock and roll!

"Take the plunge everyone," I say this all the time. Many of my clients and students are sometimes slightly put off by my enthusiasm and never-say-die attitude, but having suffered a couple of divorces, losing a brother, father and girlfriend to cancer, another love to alcoholism, never mind all of the friends that are now gone, JUST AS ALL OF YOU, I cannot help but feel great just to be alive and healthy.

Both of my daughters validate my very existence, period, not the numerous professional achievements so far. Their mother factored in greatly, of course, and her attitude towards everything was nothing short of spectacular; but, alas life moves on, and sometimes we are further blessed with a divine (in my case) gift, and she would be the previously mentioned subject of an entire volume of poetry.

Inspired? To say the very least!

Most of you are extremely successful in your various walks of life, but did you eve fail? Of course you did, unless you had a lifeline that was extraordinary.

We all lose loves, jobs and even sometimes our very dignity, which is so tough to overcome; however, if you have the heart, you have the way.

I have known some very fine musicians that would never take the real chance; either from lack of confidence (this is my main belief) and their deep-rooted and ultimate fear of failure. They remained provincial at best, never going for it all, never knowing what it's like to gather world acclaim.

Again, there is absolutely nothing wrong with this and I do honor the very notion of ultimately taking care of life.

Yes, they were respected locally, but in my case that was never enough for yours truly; and, please do not mistake me for being condescending, as I esteem all, but do not tell me that you just never had the right breaks in life...one creates them, one does not receive them!

With my career as a guitarist, I followed another set of three: "small pond", medium pond" and "big pond", and I have preached this from day one to every single one of the guitarists (600+) that I've taught.

This will expand (or should) as one develops, but in high school, for example, my "small" was my own neighborhood, my "medium" was my institution and my "large" was maybe 10-20 neighboring high schools, as word would get around and my band played everywhere.

Once I graduated from college, though, and decided to turn pro, my "big pond" was the world! You can probably figure the lesser two.

Nothing wrong with getting your ass kicked as long as you learn and acquire; I most certainly did.

The greatest analogy I can come up with is baseball, which I also played at a fairly high level.

For example, if I would lose out on seven out of ten situations, some might focus on the losses rather than the gains, and think that they were more than twice the triumphs.

If a professional baseball player has ten at bats, and gets just three hits, he has a batting average of .300. If he maintains this for an entire career, he is a Hall of Famer, and this is a fact!

Defeats are a fact of life. I laugh at them (sometimes) but always curse them, as this has forever made me feel better.

There's always the next deal, the next record, the next book, the next match, the next day. And, to participate in "the game", in my opinion, is a blessing and a privilege.

The saying is "experience can make or break you". While I agree with this conceptual statement to a point, it's never truly so extreme. Life does not start and stop on failure, nor does it with success.

Personally, I will always covet the excitement of the opportunity in trying again!

Chapter Eight

I achieved my goal of becoming a world class martial artist.

Fifteen years I ago I returned to the world of martial arts. The reason was serious; I had nearly gotten into a street fight with someone that would've ended badly for both of us, but had the wits and cunning to de-escalate this potentially life-threatening situation.

I grew up in a culture where fighting was pre-eminent. The Southern high school I attended was very provincial in its cultural evolution and these country boys were very, very tough, and I had my numerous battles at all ages...just the way it was.

I have always been on the smaller side (5'10", 150 lbs.) but was talented and intelligent enough to excel in varsity basketball, football and baseball and went on to play college "hoops" (basketball, for you that do not know).

During my higher-education days I managed to get into a few scrapes but schoolyard fights are not like the street variety; the latter can evoke serious pain and injury or worse, mainly because no one knows each other nor has any real regard for life at those moments.

The bar and street fights that I later experienced were not numerous, but occurred more than enough times to change my outlook and perspective on just how dangerous men (and women) can truly be.

I have always hated bullies, and in my youth had my fair share of dealing with them. For some strange and quite possibly "Quixotic" notion I always felt the need to deal with them, even knowing that I was going to suffer.

As well, my very own mother would champion my cause from time to time. Somehow, someway, she knew her oldest son would survive said encounters.

I started (really) boxing when I was 18 (as kids we were always putting on the gloves and pounding each other), at The New York Military Academy, where I was a camp counselor for the entire summer; and, had a former middleweight champion as my mentor. For eight straight weeks I trained with him two hours a day, five days a week. Needless to say, I took my lessons (and beatings) to heart and learned to appreciate this most gorgeous sport and its valuable skills, and my coach.

Fast forward many years, as my music career was all consuming, with concerts and touring here in America and Europe, recording, producing, seminars, summer university teaching, TV and radio appearances, etc., to when my martial arts second genesis occurred.

Once again, I somehow managed my "concept of three" into this endeavor; and, initially that was Taekwondo (the single greatest kicking art), Krav Maga (Israel's worldwide, number one regarded system of self defense) and Brazilian JiuJitsu. I felt that just one martial art wasn't enough for me and the goal of Black Belt, however I achieved, was something that I had always dreamed of.

In those 15 short years I accomplished much more, and, without boring you with my credentials here (they are presented at the end of this book), suffice it to say that the total number of Black Belts is approaching 20 as we speak.

Yes, I was committed completely, and had the requisite skill sets, but most significantly I LOVED the training, the small goals achieved on a seemingly regular basis, and the fact that I was just doing it.

I would even travel to California and Texas to qualify under martial arts masters and world champion fighters, just for the experience. An interesting side note here, often these teachers would end up as friends, as the expression goes, "like minds think alike".

Many times life just reveals itself, and as my training continued, I would find myself moving into other art forms and related disciplines and discover ancillary approaches that completed me as a martial artist and instructor.

That's the key...just getting out there and doing it!

I have been the owner/operator of **The Blue Chip Academy** for nearly a decade now and have trained many: Police, Military, US and British Special Forces, Government Security Specialists, Corporate Clients, the list goes on and on, but in truth, the most satisfaction I get is the private one-on-one instruction with men and especially women.

I previously mentioned that I have two daughters, and both have been attacked. Luckily, and with no real help from their father, as they had rarely trained with me, they survived said encounters; quite possibly their genetic disposition factored in, and very likely because of their wits and will to endure.

I have always had this disposition towards women, and will continue for the rest of my life.

It is no coincidence that God granted me two amazing daughters...best thing I've ever accomplished.

Maybe YOUR goal has always been to be a Black Belt in a particular art form. The early 70's gave us the late/great Bruce Lee and his infamous movie, "Enter The Dragon". I remember sitting in that theater thinking...WOW!

Over these last 15 years I've learned quite a lot; however, the greatest thing, again, has been the journey. Guess what? The voyage is still happening, and, most likely, always will in some capacity or another.

One of the singular and most significant aspects of self defense training is simple; it just might save your, or someone you love's, life. What a concept!

It has been empirically proven that one out of ten people in this world will actually fight back. Harsh statistics, but true, and I know this.

Some of us are born fighters, but most have to learn. I'm not talking about going out there and kicking someone's ass. This is much too dangerous. However, I preach escape and using your intelligence to live another day.

Most great instructors do exactly the same.

The street is not a playground, not a competition and most certainly not a game; it's life and death. Not trying to be dramatic, but this is how it is.

Great training teaches one to be even more adept at avoiding conflict, and I believe this is the way.

Maybe at this point in your life you want zero conflict; hello, don't we all.

I can guarantee you one thing; you find the right system/instructor and you will immediately be reborn...life will again appear more than optimistic, it will appear attainable, just like when we all were younger.

Lastly, one's age has NOTHING to do with this kind of training. I cannot tell you how many have approached me and said something to the effect of, "I'm in terrible shape...my conditioning is awful...I'm old...I'm tired...I'm inflexible..."

The excuses go on and on.

ANYONE can eventually become a Black Belt; the only thing that would preclude this is dying and all of us are much too young for that at this point of our lives.

Here's some verse created right in this very moment:

Concept of Three,

Soon you will see,

Dreams never die,

Live life, eternally.

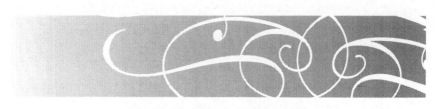

Chapter Nine

My "Professional Three"
(This is still very much evolving).

When asked what I do for a living, other than music, as my countenance (and clothes), in nearly ALL instances, quickly betrays my profession as a rock guitarist and singer, I reply that I am a creative writer (and not just an author of novels and books of poetry, but have written for numerous magazines and newspapers), and a professional martial artist.

People usually go "wow, when do you find the time?" And this brings us full circle, my friends.

I make the time, that's how I find the time.

Our lives are finite, and when we're all younger, it seems as if we have decades and decades yet to live, to experience what the world has to offer. This is true; however, and as we all now realize, time has a method of slipping away from each of us...no one is immune to this fact of life.

I believe that most of us have come to the conclusion that one of the greatest tragedies later in life is wishing that we had done something when we had the chance. How sad is lamenting the fact that you could've done this and should've done that, and now feeling it's too late?

I am a published writer, pro-athlete, and career musician (previously detailed). Not bad for a fascinating vocational "set of three", and I revolve through each of these disciplines on a nearly daily basis. They "feed" and nurture each other, never mind the supreme joy of yours truly.

I've been asked how I can "turn it on and off", especially with regards to writing. I just can, that's all; however, I do not get hung up when the creativity is not readily available to me, but rather I go for it, past the point of quitting, and usually this is fine. There are, though, times when I just bail, and that is so important with regards to not getting burned out.

Same with the most creative side of music, which is song writing and arranging. Working just past the point of "hitting the wall" is so beneficial, because it teaches one to find that often times the next step is the big one. But again, there's the point of knowing when it's not happening; guess what? The more you do, the easier to know.

Music can be a straight-up "physical" thing at times and this is when you just practice specific technical things, and this can be a very welcome relief to thinking; sort of like "musical weight lifting".

And, the same for martial arts, as the kinetic side is all too apparent; again, a comfortable respite from the cerebral aspect of things.

What keeps me going with all three of my vocational disciplines, besides my adoration for each, is my anticipation of what lies ahead, which by now in this treatise should be more than apparent to you.

Now, don't mistake this for resting on my meager laurels. For example, I have made very little at this point with my creative writing, but quite possibly with this volume (#6) and my next novel, "The Conversion of Ronnie Vee" (#7), which is well underway, I just might hit the lottery with this imaginative art; something I've truly desired for a long, long time.

Martial Arts are wonderful. They keep me in shape, maintain my flexibility and mental acuity and give me peace of mind. What more can one ask for?

I mentioned this earlier and want to again make this most emphatic point that here is no time/age limit with this discipline; far too many examples of practioners well into their 70's, 80's and even 90's. Do you suspect a correlation with this?

It's been proven that creativity gives us a distinctive health advantage.

A very astute philosopher once said that if you choose a job you love, you will never work a day in your life. Most do not have this luxury, but if your spare time is spent on what you may have once wished for, then quite possibly there will be a direct connection.

In one investigative study, with visual art the focus, researches concluded that art occupied vocational holes and sidetracked thoughts of sickness and improved well-being by decreasing damaging emotions and improving their healthy opposites.

Additionally, the impact of music, writing and art will manifest itself in your physical body. Another study, in the Journal of Psychosomatic Medicine, researchers used writing as a treatment for HIV patients and found that the act of writing actually impacted the cells in our bodies and improved immune systems.

We all need to reduce stress; this is a widely known and, obviously, empirically proven fact! Any manner in which we can accomplish this will be truly beneficial.

Make the time, take the time, to at least search for your inner-creative genius, and then see where the chips may fall. Time is one of our most treasured possessions, and the bottom half of the hourglass is slowly filling!

Lastly, sometimes life does indeed reveal itself, and offers us an additional journey.

For me, it was being contacted by Celebrity Speakers Ltd., and Celebritat Internacional Associats S.A., a worldwide speaker corporation, with offices in London, Andorra (Spain) and 18 other countries.

One of their senior consultants took a particular interest in me to join their roster of highly qualified motivational speakers, especially with specific regards to my depth as a professional and how I might impart my conceptual approach to finding and developing one's inventive intellect.

I did have the experience of hundreds of appearances in speaking to people, but most of that included music seminars, college teaching, and martial arts sessions. However, I did more than a few strictly on the various motivational aspects that were required to develop a successful music career; and, much of this was a flat out lesson in psychology!

Who knows what my future will bring? I am ready for touring the world as a professional consultant/speaker on the very nature of this book, as I emphatically believe in what I've written.

Most importantly, if I can help just one of you catch some creative light, then mission accomplished.

As I've noted several times throughout this discourse, my spiritual side is most important to me, and an ultimate goal of my evolution!

I sincerely wish all of you well.

Postscript

Without getting into too much detail, my professional life has unfolded thusly.

There will be many omissions. No matter, though, as the decades have literally melded this author's recollections into a real but vast nostalgia, but there are enough memories left over to give you a truthful picture.

How does one recall everything? It's accurately impossible, but I can assure you that my vocational voyage has been the greatest of rides and I anticipate, with boundless enthusiasm, the entire rest of my life here on earth.

Remember, use your loves of life, whatever they may be, and "touch" them with your mind, body and soul. Literally, believe in the connection of thought and process.

Search for your creative genius, it's waiting with open arms!

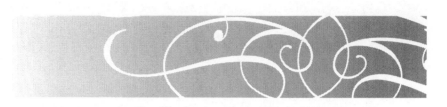

Guitarist/Composer/Singer

Solo and group instrumental and vocal records are approaching 40 (literally hundreds of songs); this includes rock fusion instrumental, rock vocal, country fusion, straight ahead jazz, jazz/rock and classical

I've guested on countless other pop, rock and roots records mainly as a guitarist and singer, and, as well, mandolin and banjo

Composed for and played on numerous commercials, radio and TV ads and shows

Have produced numerous rock, country, jazz and roots records of other artists

Three guitars in Hard Rock Cafes: 1) Washington, DC, 2) Los Angeles, CA, and one in the Caribbean

Some of the venues I've headlined in Europe and America: The Kennedy Center (DC), The Barns at Wolftrap (VA), Sarah Gould Theater (New York City), Blues Alley (DC), The Roxy (Los Angeles), The Anaheim Civic Center, Exhibition

Hall (Glasgow), The Marquee (London), Wembley Indoors (England), Music Messe (Frankfurt), and a thousand others

My corporate sponsors have totaled nearly 40

Guitar Magazine instrumentalist of the year

Current rock projects: **Here, Now and Forever**, and **RavenSong**

Internationally and critically acclaimed:

"If you love to scream when you hear Vai, Satriani, Eddie and Yngwie, it's time to be thrilled by a new scary guitar monster." *Guitar World Magazine*

"Michael Fath is quite possibly the most versatile guitarist on the planet." *Michael Angelo Batio*

"…Dazzling command of the fretboard…vividly recalls Danny Gatton's mercurial touch…memories of Joe Pass' solo virtuosity…" *The Washington Post*

"…He simply will astonish you…" *Country Plus Magazine*

"…Seasoned performer and composer…displays his wide-ranging talents and tremendous chops with a rock and roll soul and craftsman's spirit." *Guitar Player Magazine*

"…The toast of the East Coast…" *Guitarist Magazine/UK*

"…His albums are fantastic, but he's best live…the real proof is watching this American axe man performing in the flesh…" *London Music Show*

"…Virtuoso speed with an imaginative touch…" *Evening Times/Glasgow*

"…A musician's musician…instrumentalist extraordinaire…" *BAM Magazine/Los Angeles*

"Fath's arrangements and compositions are consistently compelling…impressive display of technical facility…a player with authentic jazz chops…displays a true sense of swing." *Just Jazz Guitar Magazine*

"Michael has it all, blazing chops, musical taste, and a natural sense of impeccable timing…Michael is right up there with Pass and all of the greats." *Jazz Improv Magazine*

"Michael Fath has taken the art of solo guitar to a new level of virtuosity!" *Jimmy Bruno*

www.michaelfath.com

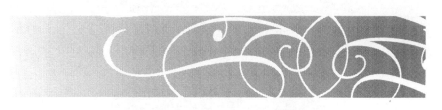

Writing Credits

2016 *28 Benedizioni di Rita* (poetry) iUniverse

2014 *Amor est Conceptualis* (poetry) iUniverse

2013 *The Village Squires – Tales of Mayhem and Revenge* (a novel) iUniverse Publishing

2010 *Reflections of Darkness and Light* (poetry) iUniverse

2009 *The Girls of Yesterday* (a novel) iUniverse

1990 - 1995 "World Guitar" - monthly column for Guitar World and Guitar School Magazines (Harris Publishing, New York, NY).

1991 - 1993 "Technique as a Result of Harmony" - monthly column for Guitarist Magazine (Music Maker Publishing, Cambridgeshire, England).

"Danny Gatton wasn't just great, he was accessible." - special request piece for The Washington Times, Oct 18, 1994.

"In Memory of Emmitt Tipton Carroll 3rd" - special request piece for Music Monthly Magazine, June 2002 (Baltimore, MD).

"Nail Those Changes" - special piece for Guitar Player Magazine (Miller Freeman Publishing, San Francisco, CA), Dec 1998.

"Geoff Thaler: Another sublime talent leaves us to wonder why!" - Special request piece for Music Monthly Magazine, November 2003 (Baltimore, MD).

(Freelance) Review/Feature for the Washington Times, Oct 2003.

Acoustic Artistry (Warner Brothers Publishing)

Hard Rock Studies/4 volumes (Hal Leonard Publishing)

Concert Solos (Cherry Lane Publishing)

J.S. Bach (Hal Leonard)

Niccolo Paganini (Hal Leonard)

Contemporary Country (Cherry Lane)\

www.michaelandrefath.com

Martial Artist

B.A. Kinesiology - Emory and Henry College, Emory, VA

Owner/operator of The Blue Chip Academy

4th degree Black Belt Master - World Taekwondo Federation

3rd degree Black Belt - World Haedong Kumdo Federation (Korean Sword)

3rd degree Black Belt – Israeli Krav Maga

3rd degree Black Belt - Israeli Kickboxing

2nd degree Black Belt - Master Martial Arts Hapkido

Brown Belt - Yang Ki Yin/Yabe Ryu JuJutsu

Blue Belt - Brazilian Gracie JiuJitsu

Muay Thai – Certified Instructor and Fighter

Apprentice Instructor - Jeet Kune Do

Professional Clients:

Washington, DC Police Force
United States Secret Service
Washington Metro Police
Alexandria, VA Police
VA State Police
Arlington County, VA Police
Loudoun County, VA Sheriff's Department
US State Department Special Ops unit
Pentagon Security Police
Marine Special Forces
INTEGRITYOne Partners
Paul Clarke - British Special Air Service
Catherine M. Reese, Esquire
Jerry Curran, Esquire

www.bluechipacademy.com

International Speaker

Currently on the roster of Celebrity Speakers Ltd. and Celebritat Internacional Associats S.A., a world leading speaker bureau, based out of London, Andorra (Spain) and numerous other countries. This journey is just beginning...

www.csaspeakers.com
www.speakers.co.uk

39244578R00066

Made in the USA
Middletown, DE
09 January 2017